PIZZA R MASTERY

2 in 1

+100 Recipes and Secrets to Master the Art of Italian Pizza Making

Antonio Savastano, Antonio Caputo

Sommario

Homemade Pizza Cookbook

50 secrets recipes from Italian master chief

Antonio Savastano

INTRODUCTION

When you think of pizza, does the word diet come to mind? Probably not! No wonder, the Italian delicacy is made up of carbohydrates and fat and therefore there is no trace of it on most diet plans. But not with the pizza diet!, believe it or not, lost over 45 kilos, is supposed to melt the pounds without giving up. But how can that be? This is easy to justify, because by satisfying your cravings with a pizza every day, the risk of food cravings decreases and you tend not to resort to other fatty or sweet temptations as quickly. "When you eat pizza, you don't need anything else. "The Italian, who lives in New York, also admits to the American Huffington Post. Conclusion: You eat fewer calories and so the pounds fall off again!

Pizza Diet: How It Works

If you opt for the pizza diet, you should be aware that you spend a little time in the kitchen during the day, because the most important principle is: No pizza from the freezer, but always freshly prepared meals. However, this is not too much of an effort, because like a conventional pizza, the dough consists of flour (it is best to use whole grain variants, as they fill you up longer), water, salt and yeast. In addition, the Italian uses a tomato sauce, fresh tomatoes, basil and mozzarella for the topping (you can use the reduced-fat variant to save a few calories). Thus, this meal has almost 600 calories and is the ideal dish for lunch.

But what is on the menu in the morning and in the evening? For breakfast, you can have fresh fruit and a portion of oatmeal, which regulates your blood sugar level and ensures that you don't feel hungry until lunch. In the evening, carbohydrates are taboo and dishes made from protein-rich meat and fish and fresh vegetables should then be on your menu so that fat burning is stimulated overnight. Of course, you should avoid sweets and alcohol during this time. With this diet, the pizza diet also works the slimming secrets of the Italians, because while a large portion of pizza, pasta and Co. can be feasted on at lunchtime, carbohydrates are banned from the table before going to bed.

BASIC RECIPE PIZZA DOUGH

Servings:2

INGREDIENTS

- 1 TL   salt
- 2 Tbsp   Olive oil (or cooking oil)
- 500 G Flour (type 00 or 480)
- 250 ml   lukewarm water
- 1 Wf Yeast (or dry yeast)
- 1 prize   sugar

PREPARATION

For the pizza dough , first sift the flour into a bowl.

Warm the water (you can also add a dash of milk here) and stir well in a bowl with the salt, a pinch of sugar, the yeast and the oil.

Now pour the liquid over the flour and knead well - first with the dough hook of a mixer and then by hand - this will make the dough smooth and supple. If the dough sticks, just add more flour.

Cover the finished dough (with a kitchen towel) and let it rest in a warm place for about 30-40 minutes - this will double its volume.

Now roll out the pizza dough on a floured work surface and top it up as you like - the dough needs about 15-25 minutes in the oven at 250 degrees, depending on the heat and topping.

MAKE PIZZA YOURSELF - BASIC RECIPE

Servings:2

INGREDIENTS

for the pizza dough

- 250 G Flour
- 0.5 Wf   Germ
- 110 ml Water, lukewarm
- 2 Tbsp   olive oil
- 1 TL salt

For the tomato sauce

- 150 G Tomatoes, peeled
- 1 Tbsp   Tomato paste

- 0.5 TL   Oregano, dried
- 1 prize   salt
- 1 prize   pepper

For the topping

- 1 prize   Oregano, dried
- 1 prize   Basil, dried
- 150 G Mozzarella
- 80 G Cheese, grated

PREPARATION

For the perfect Italian pizza dough, the flour is placed on a work surface and a well is made in the middle with your finger.

Now put the salt and olive oil into this hollow, crumble the fresh yeast into it and add a dash of warm water so that the yeast can dissolve. Cover the yeast with a little flour and let rise for a few minutes.

Then add the rest of the water and knead everything well into a dough. Put this in a bowl, cover and let rise for about 1 hour in a warm place.

In the meantime, put the peeled tomatoes (freshly blanched or canned) together with tomato paste, oregano, salt and pepper in a bowl and puree them with a hand blender.

Then you take the pizza dough, place it on a floured work surface, knead it well with your hands again, divide the dough to the desired size and roll it out thinly with a rolling pin.

Place the dough on a baking sheet lined with baking paper and brush with the tomato sauce.

Depending on your taste, top with grated cheese, mozzarella slices and black olives and season again with oregano.

Now the homemade pizza is placed in the preheated oven at 240 degrees (top / bottom heat) for about 12 minutes.

PIZZA DOUGH WITHOUT YEAST

Servings:2

INGREDIENTS

- 250 G flour smooth
- 1 Tbsp   baking powder
- 0.25 TL   salt
- 220 ml   Milk at room temperature
- 50 G Butter, room temperature

PREPARATION

Mix the flour, salt and baking powder in a large bowl.
Add the milk and butter and knead into a dough using a
mixer with a dough hook attachment.

Put some flour on the worktop and work the dough through again with your hands until it is smooth and elastic.

Either process into a sheet pizza or cut in half and form 2 pizzas out of it. Top with favorite ingredients and put in a well preheated oven at 210 degrees for 10-15 minutes.

SPICY PIZZA ROLLS

Servings:6

INGREDIENTS

- 500 G Cooked ham)
- 500 G   salami
- 3 Pc   paprika
- 200 G Cheese (grated, Edam or Gouda)
- 0.5 Pc onion
- 1 Pc   garlic
- 1 prize   basil
- 1 prize   Chilli powder
- 1 cups sour cream
- 8 Pc   Slices of white bread
- 1 prize   oregano
- 1 prize   pepper

- 1 prize   salt

PREPARATION

Cut ham, salami, paprika, onion and garlic into small pieces (dice).

Put everything in a large bowl and add 1-2 cups of sour cream, depending on the amount.

Then stir everything into a smooth mass (with a spoon), if it is still too sticky, just add some milk.

Now everything is seasoned quite heartily with salt, pepper, chilli powder etc. depending on taste and heat. Preheat the oven to 200 ° C.

Spread the white bread slices well with the mixture. Now the grated cheese is scattered on the rolls and everything is baked for about 15 minutes at 180 C.

FAST PIZZA DOUGH

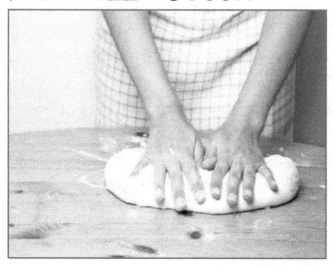

Servings:4

INGREDIENTS

- 200 ml   lukewarm milk
- 350 G Flour
- 2 Tbsp   olive oil
- 2 TL salt
- 1 Pk Dry yeast
- 1 TL sugar

PREPARATION

Mix all dry ingredients well, then use the mixer to stir in the lukewarm milk and olive oil and knead into a smooth dough.

Cover and let the dough rise in a warm place for about 1/2 hour, then roll out on a baking sheet lined with baking paper, prick several times with a fork and let it rest a little more.

Cover the pizza dough as desired and bake at 200 ° C top / bottom heat (preheated) for about 1/2 hour.

TUNA PIZZA

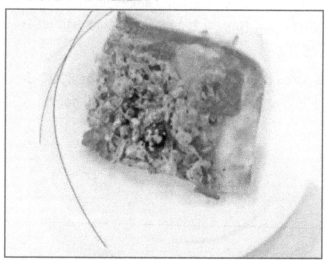

Servings:4

INGREDIENTS

- 40 G Germ
- 1 prize   salt
- 5 Tbsp   Sunflower oil
- 125 ml   Water (lukewarm)
- 500 G White flour, handy
- for the topping
- 6 Tbsp   Corn
- 190 G Tuna (can)
- 360 G Tomato sauce
- 3 Pc   Onion (red, small)
- 12 Pc Olives (black)
- 240 G Cheese (grated)

PREPARATION

Mix the flour with the water, the oil and the crumbled yeast. Add salt and knead the dough vigorously, adding more flour if necessary.

Then let it rest for half an hour to an hour in a warm place (slightly higher than room temperature). Then divide the dough into three parts and roll out into a pizza stain. Place the individual pieces on a separate baking sheet lined with baking paper.

Season the tomato sauce (salt, pepper, sugar, a little tomato paste) and spread on the dough. Top the pizzas first with the tuna, then with the onions and finally with the corn and the halved olives.

Finally, sprinkle any amount of grated cheese (possibly mozzarella) on the pizza. Then bake in the oven at approx. 190 ° C, top and bottom heat or with hot air approx. 180 ° C for approx. 15-20 minutes.

PUFF PASTRY WITH PIZZA FILLING

Servings:2

INGREDIENTS

- 100 G grated Gauda
- 250 G salami
- 250 G Ham or bacon
- 100 G Tomato paste
- 1 prize   Pizza seasoning
- 250 G Puff pastry, TK
- 1 Pc   Egg for brushing

PREPARATION

Cut the sausage into small cubes and place in a bowl with the finely chopped Gauda. Add tomato paste, pepper and pizza seasoning. Stir everything well.

Lay out the puff pastry and cut into squares. Place the filling in the center of the squares and fold the individual squares of dough into a triangle and pinch the ends together.

Brush with egg and bake in the preheated oven at 180C ° for approx. 20 minutes.

MOM'S PIZZA SAUCE

Servings:1

INGREDIENTS

- 1 Can sieved tomatos
- 2 Pc   Garlic cloves
- 5 Tbsp   Tomato paste
- 0.75 Pc   onion
- 2 Tbspolive oil
- 1 prize   pepper
- 1 prize   salt
- 1 prize   thyme
- 1 prize   basil
- 3 Tbsp   Parmesan
- 1 prize   oregano

PREPARATION

Put the tomatoes in a tall container. To do this, press the peeled garlic cloves.

Peel the onions and cut into small cubes. Add to the tomatoes together with the tomato paste. Pour in the olive oil and mix everything with the hand blender and puree until it has a creamy consistency.

Mix the parmesan into the tomato sauce.

Season with thyme, oregano, basil, salt and pepper to taste.

PIZZA ROLLS

Servings:14

INGREDIENTS

- 500 G Whole spelled flour
- 20 G Germ
- 300 ml lukewarm water
- 2 Tbsp olive oil
- 1 TL salt
- for the topping
- 1 prize salt
- 100 G Mozzarella
- 2 Pc green paprika
- 1 Pk Tomato paste
- 1 Pc onion
- 1 prize oregano

- 1 Can Tomato paste
- 1 TL   pepper
- 3 Pc   Tomatoes

for brushing

- 1 St. egg

PREPARATION

For the dough, mix the flour and 1 teaspoon salt in a bowl, crumble the yeast, knead with water and oil to form a medium-firm dough.

Leave covered in a warm place until the dough has doubled in volume. For the topping, finely chop the onion and sauté briefly in olive oil.

Cut the tomatoes and paprika, finely dice the mozzarella. Roll out the dough into a rectangle, brush with tomato paste, cover with the filling, season with salt, pepper and oregano and roll up from one side.

Cut 1-2 cm thick slices from the roll, place on a baking sheet lined with baking paper, let rise for 15 minutes.

Brush with a baked egg and bake in a preheated oven at 120 ° C for about 15 minutes.

PIZZA DOUGH WITH SPELLED FLOUR

Servings:4

INGREDIENTS

- 400 G Spelled flour
- 180 ml   Water (lukewarm)
- 1 Pk   Germ
- 1 TL   salt
- 2 Tbsp   olive oil

PREPARATION

For the pizza dough with spelled flour, mix the flour, yeast and salt in a bowl. Then slowly add the water. Add the oil. Knead the dough well with your hands until it no longer sticks.

Cover and cook in a warm place about 30 minutes let go .

Then knead again and roll out. Place on a baking sheet lined with baking paper and cover to taste.

BASIC PIZZA DOUGH RECIPE

Servings:4

INGREDIENTS

- 400 G Flour
- 1 TL salt
- 1 Pc Yeast cubes (20 grams)
- 125 ml lukewarm water
- 2 Tbsp olive oil
- 1 prize Flour, for processing
- 2 Tbsp water

for the baking sheet

- 1 Pc Parchment paper (or oil)

PREPARATION

Dissolve yeast with a little sugar in 1 dash of lukewarm water or stir until smooth.

Cover with a cloth and let rise until the surface shows cracks (15-20 minutes).

Then gradually pour in the remaining lukewarm water and the oil, working in the flour. Knead the dough until bubbles form and it comes off the edge of the bowl. Continue kneading until the dough is smooth and pliable.

Dust the dough with flour. Cover with a cloth and let rise at a good, warm room temperature until it has doubled in volume (about 30 minutes).

Line the baking sheet with parchment paper (or grease with oil). Preheat the oven to 220 degrees C. Knead the dough vigorously again.

Roll out the thinnest possible pizza base the size of the baking sheet on the floured work surface or press it flat with the ball of your hand. The edge should be a little thicker. Place on the tray and top with the topping ingredients (if desired: tomato sauce, ham, cheese, corn, etc.).

Bake the pizza in the oven (below) for 20-25 minutes at 180 ° until crispy.

PAN PIZZA

Servings:2

INGREDIENTS

- 8 Schb   salami
- 2 Pc   tomatoes
- 0.5 Pc onion
- 0.5 Can Corn
- 1 Tbsp   Oregano (dried)
- 50 G Cheese (grated)
- for the dough
- 2 Pc   Eggs
- 4 Tbsp   sour cream
- 10 Tbsp Flour (180-200 g)
- 1 prize   salt

PREPARATION

For the pan pizza, mix all the ingredients for the dough and brush a pan with oil.

Wash and slice tomatoes, peel the onion and cut into rings. Drain the corn.

Put the batter in the pan and top with tomatoes and salami. Sprinkle with oregano and lots of cheese.

Bake on a low heat for about 10 minutes. Then cover with a lid, once the cheese has melted the pizza is ready.

PIZZA DOUGH

Servings:4

INGREDIENTS

- 20 G fresh yeast
- 350 G light spelled flour
- 1 TL sea-salt
- 2 Tbsp   olive oil
- 160 ml   Water (lukewarm)

PREPARATION

Mix the flour and salt in a large bowl and make a well in the middle. Crumble in the yeast and mix with 6 tablespoons of lukewarm water.

Sprinkle some flour over it and cover with a cloth. Let the so-called fermentation test rise in a warm place for 15 minutes. The yeast batch should double its volume.

Process the fermentation sample with the remaining flour, oil and 160ml of lukewarm water to a smooth dough.

The yeast dough must be beaten until it no longer sticks. An electric mixer with a dough hook can also be used for this purpose.

Cover the dough and let it rise again until it has doubled its volume.

PIZZA DOUGH

Servings:3

INGREDIENTS

- 250 ml   Water (lukewarm)
- 1 Pk   Dry yeast
- 400 G Flour
- 1 TL   salt
- 50 ml olive oil
- 1 prize   sugar

PREPARATION

Put 100 ml of lukewarm water in a bowl. Scatter the dry yeast on top and let it rest for 2 minutes.

Add the pinch of sugar and cover the bowl in a warm place for 5-6 minutes, until the yeast starts to bubble.

Put the flour in a large bowl and pour the yeast mixture into a well.

Add the rest of the water (150 ml) and the olive oil, salt and knead with your hands.

When all the ingredients are well mixed, knead the dough for another 10 minutes until it is smooth and elastic. Then place it in an oiled bowl, cover it with household foil and place in a warm place for 2 hours.

Divide the dough and roll it out to the desired thickness on a floured work surface.

Top with the desired ingredients and bake for 20 minutes at 200 ° C.

PIZZA DOUGH WITH BAKING POWDER

Servings:4

INGREDIENTS

- 400 G Flour
- 250 ml   milk
- 3 Tbsp   olive oil
- 1 TL   salt
- 1 Pk   baking powder

PREPARATION

For the pizza dough with baking powder, put all the ingredients in a bowl and use the dough hook to form a smooth dough.

Shape a ball with your hands and roll it out on the work surface. Now cover to taste.

BASIC PIZZA DOUGH WITH CURD CHEESE

Servings: 2

INGREDIENTS

- 150 G Curd cheese
- 2 Tbsp   milk
- 50 G Vegetable oil
- 1 prize   salt
- 1 Pc   egg
- 300 G Flour
- 1 Pk   baking powder

PREPARATION

First stir the curd cheese with the milk, oil, salt and egg with a spoon until smooth.

Stir in the flour mixed with baking powder and continue working with your hand or a dough hook until the dough is smooth.

Then put in a cool place for at least an hour!

Preheat oven. (200 degrees)

Brush the dough with a mixture of tomato paste, a little water, paprika, pepper and salt.

Top it up as you like and put it in the oven.

POLENTA PIZZA

Servings:6

INGREDIENTS

- 250 G polenta
- 500 ml   water
- 250 G tomato sauce
- 0.5 Kn onion
- 200 G Mushrooms
- 100 G paprika
- 4th Schb bacon
- 150 G Gouda cheese
- 1 prize   oregano
- 2 prize   salt

PREPARATION

Bring the polenta to the boil in twice as much water and simmer for 5 minutes, stirring constantly. Then put a lid on it and let it rest for 10 minutes.

Now cut the vegetables and grate the cheese.

Put the polenta in a large, flat baking pan, spread it flat on the bottom and let it cool. Preheat the oven to 180 ° C top and bottom heat.

After the polenta has cooled, spread a thin layer of tomato sauce over the polenta base. Now sprinkle a pinch of oregano over the whole thing and place the vegetables on top of the polenta. Before sprinkling the cheese on top, salt the vegetables with 1 to 2 pinches of salt.

Put the pizza in the oven and bake for about 20 to 30 minutes.

PIZZA STICK

Servings:10

INGREDIENTS

- 1 kg   Flour
- 1 Pk   Germ
- 2 TL salt
- 0.75 milk
- 1 Tbsp   oil
- for the pizza topping
- 50 ml Tomato paste
- 50 ml Ketchup
- 6 Pc   Tomatoes, happened
- 200 G ham
- 1 prize   Pizza seasoning
- 80 G Cheese for sprinkling

PREPARATION

In a bowl, work the flour, crumbled yeast, salt, milk and oil into a dough until the dough separates from the bowl. Let the dough stand in a warm place for approx. 25-30 minutes and cover with a cloth.

Then divide the dough into 4 parts and roll out each part individually. Cut out triangles and shape smaller pizza sticks (like pretzel sticks), place on a baking sheet and flatten the top a little for the topping.

Topping: Add tomato paste, ketchup and tomato puree, finely chopped ham and pizza seasoning and stir in a bowl.

Spread the topping on the pizza sticks, sprinkle with cheese and bake in the preheated oven at 180 ° C for 15-20 minutes.

WHOLE GRAIN PIZZA DOUGH

Servings:6

INGREDIENTS

- 400 G Whole meal spelled flour
- 200 ml   Water (lukewarm)
- Pk Germ
- 0.5 TL   salt

PREPARATION

For the whole meal pizza dough, mix the flour, yeast and salt in a bowl. Then slowly add the water and knead with the dough hook of the mixer until the dough loosens from the edge of the bowl.

Cover and let rise for half an hour in a warm place. Line a baking sheet with parchment paper.

After half an hour, knead the dough well again and roll it out on the baking paper. Now cover with ingredients according to your taste.

MINI PIZZA

Servings:20

INGREDIENTS

- 250 G Flour
- 1 Tbsp   olive oil
- 1 Tbsp   Granulated sugar
- 200 ml   Water (lukewarm)
- 0.5 Pk Dry yeast
- 200 G ham
- 200 G Edam
- 1 Pc   Paprika (red)
- 250 ml   Whipped cream
- 1 prize   salt
- 1 prize   sugar
- 1 prize   Italian spices

- 20 Pc Basil leaves
- 1 prize   pepper
- 1 prize   Paprika powder

PREPARATION

Make the dough: Mix the flour, dried yeast, salt, sugar, olive oil and lukewarm water and knead very well.

Then let the dough rise in a warm place for 30 minutes.

Prepare the topping: cut the ham and cheese into small cubes (cheese can also be grated), also cut the paprika into small cubes and mix everything with the whipped cream and spices.

Knead the dough again, roll out to a thickness of approx. 1 cm and cut out circles with a diameter of 7 cm. Apply the paving compound to the circles, leaving a narrow edge free (for the sake of appearance).

Bake the mini pizzas at 200 ° C for about 15 minutes and then garnish.

PUFF PASTRY PIZZA

Servings:4

INGREDIENTS

- 1 Pc   Puff pastry (refrigerated shelf)
- 150 G salami
- 6 Tbsp Tomato paste
- 2 Tbsp   olive oil
- 3 Tbsp   water
- 3 Tbsp   Herbs (frozen)
- 1 Glass   Tomatoes (dried)
- 1 Stg leek
- 2 Pk Mozzarella
- 1 prize   pepper
- 1 prize   salt

PREPARATION

First preheat the oven for the puff pastry pizza to 180 degrees. Roll out the puff pastry with parchment paper on the baking sheet.

Mix the tomato paste with water, oil, salt, pepper and herbs and brush the dough with it.

Wash the leek and cut into rings, halve the tomatoes. Spread both on the sauce. Drain the mozzarella, cut into slices and cover with the salami.

Bake in the oven for about 20 minutes.

PIZZA WITH POTATO BATTER

Servings:4

INGREDIENTS

- 1 Wf yeast
- 500 G Potatoes (floury)
- 330 G Flour
- 1 prize   salt
- 180 ml   water
- 1 shot olive oil

for the topping

- 150 G Cooked ham)
- 40 Pc green olives
- 200 G Mozzarella
- 150 G tomatoes

- 250 G Tomatoes (happened)
- 1 prize   oregano
- 1 Tbsp   Parmesan cheese (grated)
- 1 shot Olive oil for drizzling on

PREPARATION

Potatoes in salted water, peel and press through a potato ricer and leave to cool.

Knead the yeast with the flour and the pressed potatoes, water, salt and oil to form a dough and let rise for approx. 20 minutes (= double size).

Roll out the dough, shape it and bake it in the preheated oven. approx. 15 min. at 180 ° C. Then cover with any ingredients. (e.g. tomato paste, spinach, cheese, cocktail tomatoes, olive oil to drizzle, etc.)

Then bake again in the preheated oven at 180 ° C for 15 minutes.

PIZZA WITH SPELLED FLOUR

Servings: 2

INGREDIENTS

- 300 G Spelled flour
- 1 Pk Dry yeast
- 3 Tbsp oil
- 150 ml water
- 1 TL salt
- 8 Bl ham
- 1 Can Corn
- 0.5 Pc Red peppers
- 150 G Cheese (grated)

PREPARATION

Sift the flour into a mixing bowl. Add the dry yeast, salt, oil and lukewarm water and knead to form a yeast dough. Let rest for an hour.

Place the dough on a baking tray and brush with ketchup. Place the ham on top and spread the chopped peppers and corn on top.

Sprinkle with cheese and season with oregano. Bake in the oven at 220 degrees for about half an hour until crispy.

CALZONE - PIZZA

Servings:

INGREDIENTS

- 1 Pc   Pizza dough (ready)
- 250 G Mozzarella (in cubes)
- 220 G Riccota (crumbled)
- 200 G Ham (in fine strips)
- 1 prize   oregano
- 3 Tbsp   Tomato paste

To refine4

- 2 Tr   olive oil

PREPARATION

Prepare a pizza dough .

Brush one half of the pizza with tomato paste. Cover with mozzarella, ricotta and strips of ham and season with oregano and salt. (The calzone can of course be filled with any other ingredients.)

Fold the pizza together, sprinkle the edges with water and press firmly together.

Place on a baking sheet lined with baking paper and bake in the preheated oven for approx. 20 minutes at 200 ° C.

Drizzle with olive oil to taste and serve.

PIZZA RACLETTE

Servings:8

INGREDIENTS

- 500 G Pizza dough according to the basic recipe
- 8 Tbsp   Tomatoes (happened)
- 1 TL   Pizza seasoning
- 8 Schb   ham
- 150 G Raclette cheese
- 4 Pc   Mushrooms
- 4 Tbsp   Corn

PREPARATION

The pizza dough can be prepared the day before. The next day, divide the dough into 4 portions or cut down smaller pieces, roll out and prepare the raclette pans to match the size of the raclette pan.

Stir the pizza seasoning into the tomatoes and leave to stand for about 30 minutes.

Meanwhile, place the prepared dough on a baking sheet lined with baking paper, prick with a fork and prebake at 220 degrees for about 7 minutes. (Hot air)

For the topping, cut the ham into small pieces, drain the corn and cut the mushrooms into thin slices.

Then press the pizza dough into the raclette pans. The dough shouldn't be too thick - otherwise it will take too long to finish.

Spread the tomato sauce on it and top it with the topping - finally pour the cheese over it and put it in the raclette oven - the mini pizza takes about 15 minutes to finish.

PIZZA TOAST

Servings:4

INGREDIENTS

- 8 Schb   toast
- 8 Schb   ham
- 200 G Cheese, grated
- 1 Pk   Tomato sauce
- 2 prize   salt
- 4 TL oregano
- 1 Can Corn

PREPARATION

Toast the toast slices briefly - about 2 minutes in the toaster on medium setting.

Spread tomato sauce on the toast slices. Season with salt and oregano. Top with strips of ham, corn and grated cheese.

Bake in the oven at 180 degrees.

PIZZA ROLLS

Servings:20

INGREDIENTS

- 2 Pk puff pastry
- 125 G Potting
- 4 TL Tomato paste
- 100 G salami
- 200 G Cheese, grated
- 1 prize   salt
- 2 TL oregano

PREPARATION

Mix the curd cheese with the tomato paste and season with salt and oregano. Spread the mixture on the rolled out puff pastry. Cut the salami into 1x1cm pieces and distribute evenly on the puff pastry. Scatter the cheese and roll up the puff pastry again.

Cut 1cm thick slices and place the snails on a baking sheet lined with baking paper.

Bake the snails at 200 degrees for about 20 minutes.

PIZZA WITH SPINACH LEAVES AND SHEEP CHEESE

Servings: 2

INGREDIENTS

- 300 G Flour
- 0.5 Wf   Germ
- 150 ml   lukewarm water
- 1 Tbsp   Olive oil for the dough
- 1 TL   salt
- 1 prize   sugar
- 1 Can peeled, diced tomatoes
- 2 Tbsp   olive oil
- 200 G Spinach leaves
- 1 Pc   clove of garlic

- 1 Pc   onion
- 200 G Sheep cheese
- 1 prize   freshly grated pepper
- 2 Tbsp   Flour to work out
- 2 TL Pizza seasoning

PREPARATION

Knead the flour, oil, water, crumbled yeast, sugar and salt into a smooth dough. Wrap the dough ball loosely in foil and let it rest for 30 minutes in a cool place.

Knead again and roll out into two round bases on a floured work surface. Place on a baking tray lined with baking paper. Preheat the pipe to 200 °.

Peel onion and garlic and chop finely. Sauté in the oil, add tomatoes, let simmer a little, season with pizza spice and pepper.

Wash the spinach and let it collapse dripping wet in a pan over medium heat. Dice the sheep cheese.

Spread the tomato sauce on the pizzas, prebake for about 15 minutes. Then top with spinach and sheep cheese and bake for another 10-15 minutes.

PIZZA BAGS

Servings:

INGREDIENTS

- 200 G Mushrooms
- 1 Tbsp   olive oil
- 1 Can Corn
- 1 Pc   onion
- 1 Pc   garlic
- 1 Tbsp   Herbs
- 150 G grated mozzarella
- 1 prize   salt
- 1 prize   pepper
- 1 Tbsp   Tomato paste

for the dough

- 250 G Flour
- 1 TL salt
- 0.5 cups lukewarm water
- 1 Pk Dry yeast

PREPARATION

For the dough, mix the flour a little salt, dry yeast and oregano with lukewarm water until a smooth dough is formed. Let it rest for 30 minutes from this point on.

Meanwhile, peel or wash the vegetables and cut into small pieces. Fry the onion, mushrooms, corn and garlic in a pan and then mix everything with the mozzarella and a little tomato paste. Finally, season with salt, pepper and herbs according to taste.

Cut the dough into 8 pieces of about the same size and roll out each round with a diameter of about 14 cm. Put the filling in the middle and fold up. Press the edges firmly with a fork so that nothing leaks. Then brush the bags with egg.

In the preheated oven, the pizza bags can now bake for 18 minutes at 225 degrees until golden brown.

RICE FLOUR PIZZA DOUGH

Servings:4

INGREDIENTS

- 3 G   Guar gum
- 1 Wf yeast
- 2 Tbsp   olive oil
- 350 G Rice flour
- 1 prize   salt
- 220 ml   water

PREPARATION

Mix all ingredients together very well. Cover and let the dough rise in a warm place for approx. 50 minutes.

Oil a springform pan, spread the batter over it and top it as you like.

After topping, let the dough rest for approx. 10 minutes, place in the cold oven and bake for approx. 20 minutes at 200 ° C.

NEAPOLITAN PIZZA DOUGH

Servings:6

INGREDIENTS

- 500 ml   water
- 5 G   Germ
- 25 G salt
- 850 G Flour
- 10 G   olive oil

PREPARATION

Mix the water with the salt. Add the olive oil and yeast to the water. Sift the flour into a bowl and stir in the water, olive oil, yeast and salt mixture.

Knead the dough very well with a food processor (at least 15-20 minutes) so that an elastic dough forms.

Now divide the dough into approx. 250 g portions and shape into balls. Place the balls smooth side up in a bowl or baking dish. Leave enough space in between, the dough balls will rise, then seal them airtight and let rise for 5-6 hours.

Carefully take the dough balls out of the bowl, flour them well and shape them into pizza bases with your hands. Cover according to personal taste and bake in a well preheated oven at approx. 250-300 degrees.

PIZZA HAWAII

Servings:6

INGREDIENTS

- 2 Tbsp   olive oil
- 4 Tbsp   Tomato paste
- 1 Pc   onion
- 150 G ham
- 250 G Grated cheese
- 1 prize   pepper
- 1 Can pineapple
- 1 Can Corn
- 2 Tbsp   Pizza seasoning
- 1 prize   pepper
- 1 prize   salt
- for the dough

- 0.125 warm water
- 1 Pk   Germ
- 500 G flour smooth
- 1 prize   sugar
- 2 Tbsp   olive oil
- 1 prize   salt

PREPARATION

For the pizza dough, crumble the yeast into the flour.
Add salt and sugar and knead briefly. Now slowly pour
in the water and olive oil and knead until the dough
comes off the edge.

The dough must now rest covered for half an hour.
Then put some flour on the work surface and roll out
the dough as large as the sheet is. Brush the tray with
oil and place the dough on top. Pierce holes with a fork.

Brush the dough with tomato paste and spread the olive
oil on top. Top with sliced onion, then the ham and half
of the grated cheese. Season with salt and pepper.

Now distribute the pineapple and the rest of the
cheese on top and sprinkle with pizza seasoning. Now
bake at 230 degrees bottom heat for 15 minutes.

POLENTA PIZZA

Servings:4

INGREDIENTS

- 750 ml   Soup
- 1 Tbsp   butter
- 250 G polenta
- 2 Can Tomatoes (diced)
- 200 G Mozzarella
- 120 G salami
- 3 Tbsp   Herbs (frozen)
- 1 Tbsp   olive oil
- 1 prize pepper
- 1 prize   salt

PREPARATION

For the polenta pizza, first preheat the oven to 200 degrees and line the baking sheet with baking paper.

Bring the soup and butter to a boil in a saucepan. Add the polenta and let it soak over a low heat for 20 minutes. Stir frequently.

Spread the polenta 2 cm thick on the prepared tray. Top with the tomatoes. Cut the mozzarella into pieces, cut the salami into strips and distribute evenly on the pizza. Season with salt and pepper. Sprinkle the herbs on top. Drizzle with the olive oil.

Bake in the oven for 25 minutes.

PIZZA SCHNITZEL

Servings: 4

INGREDIENTS

- 3 Pc   Tomatoes (sliced)
- 4 TL   Pizza seasoning
- 200 G Pizza cheese (grated)
- 4 Schb   ham
- 4 Pc   Pork, veal or turkey schnitzel
- 1 prize   salt
- 1 shot Oil for the pan
- 1 prize   pepper
- 2 Tbsp   Tomato paste

PREPARATION

Briefly fry the salted and peppered schnitzel in a pan with a dash of oil.

Place the pieces of meat on a tray and, like a pizza, thinly cover with the tomato paste, ham and tomato slices, depending on your taste. Sprinkle with the pizza cheese and pizza seasoning and bake in the stove for about 15-25 minutes at 180 ° in the preheated oven.

Serve with rice and a green salad.

LOW CARB PIZZA

Servings:4

INGREDIENTS

- 300 G cauliflower
- 200 G Cheese (grated)
- 2 Pc Eggs
- 0.5 TL   salt
- 1 Tbsp   olive oil
- 1 Tbsp   olive oil

for the topping

- 1 Pc Zucchini (medium)
- 2 Can tuna
- 1 Pc Spring onion
- 2 Tbsp   Oregano (dried)

- 0.5 Federation   Asparagus (green)
- 3 Tbsp   Tomato sauce
- 1 prize   pepper
- 1 prize   salt

PREPARATION

For the low carb pizza preheat the oven to 200 degrees. Wash and clean the cauliflower and chop very finely in the food processor.

Mix with the remaining ingredients to form a dough and spread it on a baking sheet lined with baking paper. Brush with olive oil and tomato sauce and bake for 20 minutes.

Wash the asparagus, clean and cook in salted water until al dente.

For the topping: Wash and clean the zucchini and cut into thin slices. Season the tomato sauce with salt, pepper, spring onion and oregano, stir well.

Spread the tomato sauce on the dough, sprinkle with zucchini slices and asparagus and put in the oven for another 15 minutes. Fresh basil leaves can be used as a decoration before serving.

POLENTA PIZZA

Servings:4

INGREDIENTS

- 250 G Corn grits
- 2 Tbsp   Cornmeal
- 1 prize   salt
- 1 Tbsp   Sunflower oil
- water

PREPARATION

Bring about 1 liter of water to the boil. Add salt and sprinkle in the corn grits. Cook for about 1/4 hour over low heat and add the corn flour.

Cook for another 10 to 15 minutes, stirring constantly, until the porridge separates from the bottom.

Spread the polenta about 2 cm thick on an oiled baking sheet while it is still hot. Cool for about 1 hour and allow to set.

Preheat the oven to 220 ° C. Top the polenta as desired and bake the polenta pizza for about 15 minutes.

PIZZA POT BATTER

Servings: 4

INGREDIENTS

- 200 G Potting
- 1 Pc egg
- 4 Tbsp milk
- 8 Tbsp oil
- 1 Msp salt
- 0.5 Pk baking powder
- 200 G Flour

PREPARATION

For the pizza dough, knead the quark, egg, milk, oil, salt, flour and baking powder in a bowl to form a smooth dough.

Then roll out on the work surface and further process or cover as desired.

PIZZA DOUGH

Servings:1

INGREDIENTS

- 500 G wheat flour
- 2 Tbsp   olive oil
- 1 Wf   yeast
- 1 prize   salt
- 1 prize   sugar
- 200 ml   Water (lukewarm)

PREPARATION

Weigh the salt, sugar, and olive oil into the bowl of the food processor. Then weigh the flour on top and only now the yeast (important: yeast must never come into contact with salt, salt kills the yeast. Therefore, salt at the bottom and the yeast at the top.) Then add the water and the dough with the Mix the food processor on a low setting. Once the dough has been mixed well, increase the level and "mix" or knead the dough intensively.

A dough is ready when you can test the dough. That means you take a small piece of the dough and carefully pull it apart, alternately pulling it apart in a circle. The dough in the middle must be able to be drawn very thinly without tearing, so thin that you can read a newspaper through it. Only then is the dough finished and the glue processed accordingly.

Now let the dough rest for two hours in a covered bowl. Knead once or twice in between and let rest again. (It would be better to let the dough rest in the refrigerator for 6-8 hours and then knead again briefly from time to time.)

After the resting phase, roll out the dough in a circle, let it rest briefly every now and then so that the glue (glue: proteins that hold the dough together) can relax and the dough can then be processed more easily. Shape approx. 25-30 cm round pizza. Place the pizza sauce and the remaining topping on top and place in the preheated oven.

MINIATURE PIZZAS

Servings:8

INGREDIENTS

- 200 G wheat flour
- 200 G Spelled flour
- 1 Pk   baking powder
- 1 prize   salt
- 90 ml olive oil

for the topping

- 8 Pc Cherry tomatoes
- 4 Schb   Salami (small)
- 8 Tbsp   Sieved tomatos
- 110 G Parmesan

PREPARATION

For the dough, 60 g of parmesan are grated and mixed with the two types of flour, the baking powder and 1 teaspoon of salt in a bowl. With 90 ml of oil and 250 ml of water, everything is kneaded into a smooth dough. The dough is kneaded on a floured work surface for about 2-3 minutes. Then you can wrap it in cling film and let it rest for 30 minutes.

You can now preheat the oven to 200 degrees.

Now the dough is rolled out to a thickness of approx. 2 mm on a lightly floured work surface and 8 dwarf pizzas with a diameter of 12 cm are cut out.

The cherry tomatoes are cut into slices. The salami is cut down into small pieces.

Then the pizzas are coated with 1 tablespoon each of the tomato strains and sprinkled with the cheese.

Now you can top 4 pizzas with cherry tomatoes and 4 pizzas with salami. Place the pizzas on a parchment-lined baking sheet. They are baked on the middle rack for 6-8 minutes, until the batter is golden brown and the cheese bubbles.

Now you can take the pizzas out of the oven and arrange them.

WHOLE GRAIN PIZZA BUNS

Servings:10

INGREDIENTS

- 900 G Whole spelled flour
- 30 G Germ
- 150 G Parmesan
- 0.25 cream
- 0.25 red wine
- 0.25 water
- 1 Pc Egg to brush
- 5 Bl ham
- 6 Pc Olives
- 1 Pc tomatoes
- 1 Pc paprika
- 1 prize oregano

- 1 Pc   garlic
- 1 shot Oil to sauté
- 1 prize   pepper
- 1 prize   salt

PREPARATION

Prepare a dough with the specified ingredients, roll it out, top it with cheese or ham, olives, etc. Beat the dough over it. Brush with egg and let rise. Bake at 250 degrees for about 12 minutes.

FINE PIZZA SNAILS

Servings:50

INGREDIENTS

- 760 G Flour
- 400 ml   milk
- 160 G butter
- 1 Wf Germ
- 1 TL   salt
- 1 TL   sugar
- 1 Pk   Pizza cheese (grated)

for the fullness

- 500 G Tomato (happened)
- 3 Pc   Garlic cloves
- 1 prize   salt

- 1 TL   Pizza seasoning
- 250 G Toasted ham

PREPARATION

For the dough, put milk and butter in a small saucepan and heat until the butter melts. Let cool down briefly.

Sift the flour into a mixing bowl, stir in the salt, sugar and crumbled yeast. Pour the milk-butter mixture over the flour and knead with the dough hook of the food processor until a smooth dough is formed. Leave the dough in the bowl, cover with a kitchen towel and let rise until it is about twice its size.

Press the garlic for the filling, cut the ham into very small cubes. Then mix all ingredients together in a bowl.

Divide the dough into 4 parts. Roll out the first dough as rectangular as possible on a floured work surface. Cover with a quarter of the fullness (leave a few centimeters free at the edge). Roll up and cut into slices.

Cover a baking sheet with parchment paper and place the pizza slices on top. Lightly press. Bake in the oven at 180 ° C for about 20 minutes.

Do the same with the rest of the batter and the filling.

PIZZA AL PROSCIUTTO

Servings:4

INGREDIENTS

- 200 G   cooked ham
- 200 G Mozzarella
- 1 shot olive oil
- 1 Pc   Pizza dough (ready)
- 1 Can Pizza sauce (or tomato sauce)
- 1 prize   pepper
- 1 prize   salt

PREPARATION

Brush the pizza dough with olive oil, then brush with tomato sauce. Now top with the ham cut into small cubes.

Cut the mozzarella cheese into slices and cover the pizza with it. Drizzle with a little olive oil and bake in the preheated oven (180 ° C, Th. 7) for 25 minutes.

SEAFOOD PIZZA

Servings:4

INGREDIENTS

- 500 G Mussels, fresh
- 250 G Shrimp, frozen
- 200 G tomatoes
- 200 G Mozzarella
- 2 Tbsp   olive oil
- 1 Pc   Pizza dough, finished product
- 1 prize   oregano
- 1 prize   pepper
- 1 prize   salt

PREPARATION

Roll out the pizza dough and brush with olive oil.

Cook the mussels in a little butter in a large saucepan for 10 minutes and remove the shells.

Place tomatoes in boiling water for about 1-2 minutes, then peel and cut into small pieces. Cover the dough with the tomatoes.

Salt and pepper the pizza and spread the seafood on top. Put the sliced mozzarella cheese on top, drizzle some olive oil over it and sprinkle with a pinch of oregano. Then bake in the oven at 180 ° Celsius for 20 to 25 minutes.

PIZZA DOUGH WITHOUT YEAST

Servings:4

INGREDIENTS

- 150 G Potting
- 300 G Flour
- 50 ml milk
- 50 ml olive oil
- 1 Pc Eggs
- 1 TL salt
- 1 Pk baking powder

PREPARATION

You need a large bowl for the pizza dough without yeast. Mix all of the specified ingredients together, this is best done with your hands.

Then roll out the dough and top it as you like.

SIMPLE PIZZA ROLLS

Servings:4

Ingredients

- 1 Can Pizza tomatoes
- 200 G cooked ham (diced)
- 200 G Salami (dicing)
- 200 G grated cheese
- 150 G sour cream
- 1 Pa Buns / rolls / toast slice

PREPARATION

Mix all ingredients well and season with pizza seasoning.
Then spread the mixture on halved rolls or slices of
toast.

Cover with Scheibletten cheese and put in the preheated oven for at least 15 minutes.

PIZZA BAG

Servings: 4

INGREDIENTS

- 400 G Pizza dough, finished product
- 100 G Tomatoes, chunky, can
- 2 Tbsp   Olive oil
- 1 TL   Oregano, dried
- 1 prize   salt
- 1 prize   pepper
- 100 G Mozzarella, grated
- 200 G Minced beef
- 1 Pc   Onion, small

PREPARATION

Peel the onion and cut into fine cubes. Heat the olive oil in the pan and first add the onion pieces, then the minced meat and fry until it is crumbly. Stir in the tomatoes and season to taste with salt, pepper and oregano. Simmer over low heat for 10 minutes.

Preheat the oven to 200 ° C and line a baking sheet with baking paper.

Roll out the pizza dough, cut into 8 squares and place on the baking sheet. Divide the filling between the pieces of dough. Then fold the squares together to form triangles and press down the edges.

Bake the pizza pots until golden brown, which takes about 12 minutes. After 10 minutes, sprinkle with the cheese and take it out of the oven if it has run.

PIZZA WITH SPINACH AND EGG

Servings:2

INGREDIENTS

- 250 G Pizza flour
- 125 ml   Water (lukewarm)
- 0.5 Wf   Germ (fresh)
- 1 prize   sugar
- 1 Tbsp   olive oil
- 0.5 TL   salt
- 1 Cup Flour to work with
- 200 G Pizza cheese (grated)
- 400 G Spinach leaves (frozen)
- 1 Pc   onion

- 1 Pc   garlic
- 1 Tbsp   butter
- 4 Pc   Eggs
- 150 G Tomato sauce according to the basic recipe
- 1 prize   pepper
- 1 prize   salt

PREPARATION

Thaw the frozen spinach leaves in a bowl. For the pizza dough, put lukewarm water in a mixing bowl and dissolve the yeast and sugar in it.

Then knead with the flour, olive oil and salt to form a smooth dough, shape it into a ball, dust with flour, cover with cling film and let it rest until it has risen twice as high.

During this time, peel the onion and garlic, chop them finely and let them soften in butter. Squeeze the thawed spinach leaves well, add, sauté briefly, season with salt and pepper and let cool a little.

Roll out the risen pizza dough thinly, brush with the tomato sauce , sprinkle with pizza cheese and top with the spinach leaves. With a soup spoon, press the pizza in a little in four places and place a cracked egg in each of the resulting hollows.

To bake the pizza, bring the pizza stone in the oven to the highest possible temperature, place the pizza on top and bake for 4-5 minutes until crispy.

PIZZA ALLA NAPOLETANA

Servings:4

INGREDIENTS

- 400 G tomatoes
- 100 G Anchovy fillets
- 200 G Mozzarella
- 1 shot olive oil
- 1 prize   oregano
- 1 prize   salt
- 1 prize   pepper
- 1 Pk   Pizza dough

PREPARATION

Brush the rolled out pizza dough with olive oil and cover
with the peeled, chopped tomatoes. To do this, place

them in boiling water for 1-2 minutes, then the skin can be peeled off more easily.

Cut the cheese into small cubes and spread over the dough with the anchovy fillets. Drizzle with a little olive oil, season with salt, pepper and sprinkle with oregano. Bake in the preheated oven at 180 ° C top / bottom heat for 5 minutes.

GREEK PIZZA

Servings:4

INGREDIENTS

- 500 G Flour (type 00 or 480)
- 1 prize   salt
- 2 Tbsp   olive oil
- 250 ml   Water (lukewarm)
- 1 Wf Germ (41g)
- 1 Tbsp   olive oil
- for the topping
- 2 Pc Peppers (green)
- 2 Pc Onion (red, small)
- 4 Pc Cocktail tomatoes
- 100 G Feta
- 8 Pc Olives (black and green, pitted)
- 150 G Tomato sauce
- 80 G Broccoli florets (TK)

For brushing

- 1 Tbsp   olive oil

PREPARATION

For the Greek pizza, first prepare a pizza dough. Put the flour, salt, oil and lukewarm water in a bowl.
Crumble the yeast, then knead everything into a smooth dough. Then cover with a kitchen towel and let stand at room temperature for at least 30 minutes.

In the meantime, prepare the pizza topping, wash the cocktail tomatoes from the greens and cut them into quarters. Peel the small red onions in quarters and separate them into individual onion layers. Cut the peppers into strips. Wash and drain broccoli florets. Drain the feta and cut into cubes. Drain the olives in a colander.

Then knead the dough again briefly and cut in half. Roll out every single piece of dough with a rolling pin, pulling up one edge of the dough. Spread the tomato sauce thickly and distribute the individual prepared ingredients for the topping on the pizza. Brush the pizza edge with olive oil.

Place the pizzas separately on a baking tray lined with baking paper and fry them in the preheated oven at 180 ° C with hot air for about 20 minutes until crispy.

MILLET PIZZA

S

Servings:4

INGREDIENTS

- 150 G millet
- 3 Tbsp   Sunflower oil
- 500 ml   water
- 1 prize   salt

PREPARATION

Bring about 1/2 l of water to the boil. Add salt. Add the millet and cook for about 1/4 hour until soft.

Stir in 2 tbsp sunflower oil.

Lightly oil a springform pan (approx. 22 cm diameter).

Press the millet into a springform pan while it is still warm, pull up the edge a little.

Top the millet pizza as desired. Preheat the oven to 200 ° C and bake the millet pizza for about 30 minutes.

CONCLUSION

Pizza is certainly the best-known and for many also the most popular dish from Italy. The flatbread from the Neapolitan cuisine made its triumphant advance on the menus of the world at the beginning of the 19th century.

The most important thing in a pizza recipe is to use the right pizza dough and fresh ingredients for the topping. But the right baking time and the right baking device (pizza oven) should not be neglected either - here you will find a selection of pizza recipes that are easy to make yourself.

PIZZA RECIPES

+50 Recipes and Secrets to Master the Art of Italian Pizza Making

Antonio Caputo

Disclaimer

The information contained i is meant to serve as a comprehensive collection of strategies that the author of this eBook has done research about. Summaries, strategies, tips and tricks are only recommendation by the author, and reading this eBook will not guarantee that one's results will exactly mirror the author's results. The author of the eBook has made all reasonable effort to provide current and accurate information for the readers of the eBook.

INTRODUCTION

When you think of pizza, does the word diet come to mind? Probably not! No wonder, the Italian delicacy is made up of carbohydrates and fat and therefore there is no trace of it on most diet plans. But not with the pizza diet!, believe it or not, lost over 45 kilos, is supposed to melt the pounds without giving up. But how can that be? This is easy to justify, because by satisfying your cravings with a pizza every day, the risk of food cravings decreases and you tend not to resort to other fatty or sweet temptations as quickly. "When you eat pizza, you don't need anything else. "The Italian, who lives in New York, also admits to the American Huffington Post. Conclusion: You eat fewer calories and so the pounds fall off again!

Pizza Diet: How It Works

If you opt for the pizza diet, you should be aware that you spend a little time in the kitchen during the day, because the most important principle is: No pizza from the freezer, but always freshly prepared meals. However, this is not too much of an effort, because like a conventional pizza, the dough consists of flour (it is best to use whole grain variants, as they fill you up longer), water, salt and yeast. In addition, the Italian uses a tomato sauce, fresh tomatoes, basil and mozzarella for the topping (you can use the reduced-fat variant to save a few calories). Thus, this meal has almost 600 calories and is the ideal dish for lunch.

But what is on the menu in the morning and in the evening? For breakfast, you can have fresh fruit and a portion of oatmeal, which regulates your blood sugar level and ensures that you don't feel hungry until lunch. In the evening, carbohydrates are taboo and dishes made from protein-rich meat and fish and fresh vegetables should then be on your menu so that fat burning is stimulated overnight. Of course, you should avoid sweets and alcohol during this time. With this diet, the pizza diet also works the slimming secrets of the Italians, because while a large portion of pizza, pasta and Co. can be feasted on at lunchtime, carbohydrates are banned from the table before going to bed.

PIZZA STICKS ACCORDING TO A FAMILY RECIPE

Servings:5

INGREDIENTS

- 12 Pc Aufbackbrötchen
- 0.125 kg   butter
- 1 Pc   egg
- 200 G grated cheese
- 2 Pc   garlic
- 200 G ham
- 1 Pk   Potting
- 1 Pc   paprika
- 1 Federation parsley

- 1 shot Lime juice
- 1 shot Grand manner

PREPARATION

Cut the ham and possibly paprika into small pieces.

Mix the curd cheese and butter until foamy - add the ham, cheese, parsley, egg and pressed garlic. Mix well.

Halve the rolls and place the pizza mixture on top. Just put it in the oven for 15-20 minutes and you're done.

PIZZA ROLLS

Servings:1

INGREDIENTS

- 10 G salt
- 250 ml   Tomato paste
- 2 Tbsp   olive oil
- 0.5 Pc onion
- 1 Pc   clove of garlic
- 2 TL oregano
- 150 G Cheese (grated)

for the dough

- 500 G Flour
- 1 Tbsp   Baking malt

- 300 ml   water
- 5 G Germ
- 2 Tbsp   oil
- 1 TL sugar

PREPARATION

First put the flour in a bowl and add the yeast, oil, salt and baking malt. Knead into a smooth dough with the water and let rest for 1 hour.

In the meantime, heat the olive oil in a saucepan and roast the finely chopped onion and garlic in it. Add the tomato paste and let it simmer for 15 minutes. Add the sugar and oregano and season with salt and pepper.

Shape the dough into small Schifferl and place the tomato sauce in the middle. Finally, sprinkle the cheese on top, place on a baking sheet lined with baking paper and bake the rolls at 210 degrees Celsius for about 15 minutes.

QUICK PIZZA ROLLS

Servings:6

INGREDIENTS

- 200 G Salami (dicing)
- 200 G Ham (dicing)
- 2 Pc Onion (finely chop)
- 2 Pc   Paprika (diced)
- 200 G Cheese (grated)
- 8 Pc Toast slices (or white bread)

PREPARATION

Mix all ingredients well and only add salt, pepper and possibly basil to taste.

Then spread the mixture on slices of toast or white bread and bake for about 20 minutes.

TURKISH PIZZA

Servings:8

INGREDIENTS

- 500 G Minced lamb / beef
- 1 Pc   onion
- 4 Pc   Garlic cloves
- 1 Can Tomatoes (cubes with juice)
- 2 Tbsp   Tomato paste
- 1 Tbsp   Paprika powder
- 0.5 TL   Cumin (ground)
- 1 Tbsp   Lemon juice
- 20 G Parsley (finely chopped)
- 3 Tbsp   olive oil
- 1 prize   salt

- 1 prize   pepper

Dough

- 20 G Germ
- 500 G plain flour
- 40 ml olive oil
- 2 TL Salt (for the dough)
- 1 prize   sugar

PREPARATION

We start with the dough: To do this, dissolve the yeast in a little water. The flour is kneaded well with oil, salt, sugar and the yeast mixture. Cover with a damp cloth and let the pizza dough rise for about an hour.

Next, prepare the sauce: peel and finely chop the onions and garlic. Sweat in a saucepan with 2 tablespoons of olive oil. This is where the minced meat is added and is fried through.

Add the tomatoes with sauce and tomato paste and cook everything together on medium heat for about 15 minutes. Seasoned with paprika powder, cumin, lemon juice, salt, pepper and parsley, the sauce is ready.

The oven is preheated to 220 ° C and baking sheets are prepared with baking paper.

After resting, the dough is kneaded again and eighthed. Roll out the pieces in an oval shape so that 2-3 pieces fit on a tray.

The finished sauce is spread on top and baked in the oven for about 15 minutes.

PIZZA DOUGH

Servings:1

INGREDIENTS

- 450 G Flour
- 1.5 TL salt
- 4 Tbsp   olive oil
- 0.30 water
- 1 Pk yeast

PREPARATION

First you put the flour and salt in a large bowl and mix them together.

Put the oil, the yeast (it is best to crumble the yeast in your warm hands at room temperature) and the warm water (not hot !!) in a smaller container. The mixture is stirred well with a fork.

Finally, put the yeast mass in the large bowl and carefully stir everything with a dough hook.

Then you cover the bowl and let the dough rise in a warm place for a good hour.

PIZZA RING

Servings:2

INGREDIENTS

- 2 Pc onion
- 3 Pc   tomatoes
- 1 Pc   Paprika (green)
- 1 prize   oregano
- 1 kg   Pizza dough (ready or fresh)
- 100 G Ham sausage
- 100 G cheese
- 100 G Tomato paste
- 1 prize   pepper
- 1 prize   salt

PREPARATION

Finely dice the onion. Dice tomatoes, peppers, ham sausage and cheese as well.

Put a dash of oil in a pan and steam the onion until translucent and allow to cool. Mix the ingredients for the filling (onion, bell pepper, tomatoes, ham, cheese, salt, pepper, oregano) in a bowl.

Roll out the pizza dough and cut out individual rectangles (approx. 20x8 cm) with the pizza wheel.

Line a round shape or a baking sheet with parchment paper or brush with butter. Then lay the individual rectangular parts all around, edge to edge. Then place it again edge to edge above individual rectangles.

Now the lower half is coated with tomato paste and filled with the previously prepared filling. Then close the rectangular parts or the ring one after the other. Press the dough down a little until you get a nice ring. Brush with egg and sprinkle with cheese and spices if desired.

Bake in the preheated oven at 180 ° hot air or top and bottom heat for 20-25 minutes until golden yellow.

POLENTA PIZZA WITH VEGETABLES

Servings:2

INGREDIENTS

- 0.5 TL   salt
- 80 G polenta
- 1 Msp nutmeg
- 1 prize   pepper
- 3 Tbsp   sour cream
- 200 ml   water

for the topping

- 2 Pc   tomatoes

- 1 Pc Paprika (red)

PREPARATION

For the polenta pizza with vegetables, first preheat the oven to 200 degrees. Bring a saucepan with about 200 ml salt water to a boil. Stir in polenta and season with nutmeg and pepper.

Cook the polenta over a low heat for about 5 minutes, stirring constantly. As soon as it thickens, stir in the sour cream and season again. Take off the stove and let cool down a bit.

In the meantime, wash the tomatoes and peppers and cut them into short strips. Dice the aubergines.

Line a cake tin with baking paper and spread the polenta on it with a spatula. Spread the vegetables on top.

Bake in the oven for about 25 minutes.

PIZZA SAUCE WITH HERBS

Servings:1

INGREDIENTS

- 1 Can Tomatoes (in pieces)
- 4 Tbsp   Tomato paste
- 1 Pc onion
- 1 Pc clove of garlic
- 1 prize   sugar
- 150 ml   broth
- 1 TL Herbs (basil / oregano)
- 3 Tbsp   Olive oil for the pan
- 1 prize   Cayenne pepper
- 1 prize   pepper
- 1 prize   salt

PREPARATION

For the pizza sauce, first peel and finely chop the onion and garlic. Wash the tomatoes and also cut them into small pieces.

Then heat the oil in a heavy pan and sauté the onion until translucent, add the garlic and sauté briefly.

Now add the small pieces of tomato and pour the soup broth (clear vegetables or meat soup) over it - stir in the tomato paste and simmer briefly.

Add any finely chopped herbs (such as basil, oregano, marjoram,) and season with salt and pepper. Simmer gently for about 10-15 minutes and then season again to taste.

SALAMI PIZZA

Servings:3

INGREDIENTS

- 500 G Flour
- 1 Pk Dry yeast
- 1 TL salt
- 1 TL Granulated sugar
- 70 ml olive oil
- 300 ml   lukewarm water
- 20 Schb salami
- 1 Pk Mozzarella
- 3 Tbsp   Tomato puree

PREPARATION

Sift the flour into a mixing bowl and mix with the dry yeast, salt and sugar.

Add the olive oil and water and knead everything into a dough. Let rest for 1 hour.

Then place on a baking sheet lined with baking paper so that the edge is slightly thicker than the rest of the base.

Pre-bake in the oven at 240 degrees for 10 minutes, remove and brush with the tomato puree.

Then spread the sliced mozzarella on top and top with the sliced salami.

Season with oregano and bake in the oven at 240 degrees until the edge is nice and brown.

TIN PIZZA WITH SARDINES AND CAPERS

Servings:4

INGREDIENTS

- 250 G Flour
- 1 Pk   Dry yeast
- 50 G   butter
- 1 Pc   Egg yolk
- 70 ml milk
- 1 prize   salt
- 250 G Tomato paste
- 1 Pc   Garlic cloves
- 1 prize   Salt

- 1 Msp pepper
- 150 G Pizza cheese
- 1 TL   Pizza seasoning
- 2 Can Sardines
- 3 Tbsp   Capers
- 1 Can Corn
- 200 G Mushrooms

PREPARATION

Mix the flour with salt and dry yeast, stir in the yolk, lukewarm butter and the lukewarm milk, knead into a smooth dough with a food processor. Cover with a kitchen towel and let rise for 30 minutes.

In the meantime, peel and finely chop the garlic. Clean and slice the mushrooms, drain the sardines and cut into pieces. Drain the corn through a sieve.

Roll out the pizza dough on a work surface dusted with flour and place on a baking sheet lined with baking paper. Mix the tomato paste with the garlic, salt and pepper and spread on the pizza dough.

Cover the pizza with sardines, capers, corn and mushrooms, sprinkle with pizza seasoning and pizza cheese and bake in the preheated oven at 200 degrees for 15-20 minutes.

PIZZA DOUGH WITHOUT YEAST

Servings:4

INGREDIENTS

- 240 G Potting
- 260 G Flour
- 0.5 TL   salt
- 1 Pc   egg
- 1 Pk   baking powder

PREPARATION

Mix the flour and baking powder and sift into a bowl. Add the egg, curd cheese and salt and quickly knead everything into a smooth dough.

Grease the baking sheet and roll out the dough on it. Cover the dough sheet as you like and bake for about 20 minutes at 220 ° C, depending on the thickness of the topping.

BREAD MIX PIZZA

Servings:4

INGREDIENTS

- 2 Tbsp   Whole wheat flour for work surface
- 250 G Feta cheese
- 250 ml   Tomato sauce
- 4 Tbsp   Tomato ketchup (spicy)
- 6 Schb   Smoked ham
- 1 Tbsp   oregano
- 2 Tbsp   olive oil
- 1 Pk   Six grain bread mix
- 1 prize   basil
- 2 Pc   Peppers (green)

- 2 Pc   Tomatoes (medium)
- 1 prize   pepper
- 1 prize   salt

PREPARATION

Mix the baking mixture with warm water according to the instructions and let rise for 40 minutes. Mix the tomato sauce with the tomato ketchup, spices, salt, pepper and olive oil.

Crumble the feta cheese and cut the ham into strips. Preheat the oven to 200 degrees. Cover the baking sheet with baking paper. Roll out the dough to the size of a sheet.

Brush with the seasoned tomato sauce. Place the ham, feta, tomatoes, peppers on top and bake in the oven for 20-25 minutes.

PIZZA SAUCE

S

Servings:6

INGREDIENTS

- 2 Tbsp   Dressing sauce
- 1 Tbsp   vinegar
- 1 TL   oregano
- 5 Tbsp   strained tomato sauce
- 2 Tbsp   Triplo
- 1 TL   Vegeta
- 3 Tbsp   water

PREPARATION

Roll out the finished pizza dough on a baking sheet lined with baking paper.

For the pizza topping, stir the dressing sauce, vinegar, oregano, tomato sauce, triplo, vegeta and water in a bowl for about 1 minute, brush the pizza dough with it and bake in the oven for 20-25 minutes.

MANAKISH

Servings:2

INGREDIENTS

- 1 Pk   Dry yeast
- 500 G Flour
- 1 TL   Salt (deleted)
- 1 TL   Sugar (deleted)
- 5 Tbsp   olive oil
- 200 ml   Water (lukewarm)
- 1 Tbsp   Olive oil for brushing

for seasoning and coating

- 2 Tbsp   Zatar (spice mixture)
- 100 ml   olive oil

PREPARATION

For the Manakish recipe, first put the water, sugar and yeast in a small bowl and mix everything together well. Let stand a few minutes at room temperature.

Put the flour (sifted) and salt in a bowl, make a well and add the yeast mixture. Add olive oil. Knead everything into a fine dough. (Kitchen machine). Shape the dough into a ball, brush with oil and cover with a cloth and let rise for about 50 minutes until the dough has doubled.

Mix the zatar spice mixture and olive oil. Divide the dough into 6 pieces, form small pizzas and brush with zatar oil.

Top the pizzas with other ingredients as desired, place on a baking tray lined with baking paper and bake in the preheated oven for about 7-8 minutes, top and bottom heat until golden brown.

PIZZA DOUGH

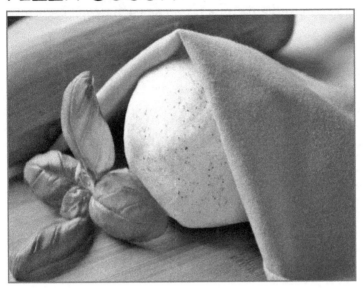

Servings:1

INGREDIENTS

- 450 G Flour
- 2 Pc Eggs
- 3 prize   salt
- 120 G margarine
- 0.5 Pk Dry yeast
- 2 Tbsp   oregano
- 2 Tbsp   oil

PREPARATION

Preheat the oven to 180 degrees.

Mix the dry yeast with lukewarm water and add the remaining ingredients, mix into a smooth dough and roll out.

Line the baking sheet, which has been greased with oil, with the dough and cover as desired. Then bake for 20 minutes.

LENTIL PIZZA

Servings: 3

INGREDIENTS

- 1 Pk   Pizza dough (basic recipe)
- 1 Can lenses
- 1 Pc   onion
- 200 G Mozzarella
- 2 TL   curry
- 200 G yogurt
- 1 prize   pepper
- 1 prize   salt

PREPARATION

Preheat the oven to 220 degrees. Roll out the dough on a baking sheet with baking paper.

Peel the onion and cut into rings, drain the lentils. Cut the mozzarella into cubes.

Spread the yogurt on the dough. Spread the lentils, onions and mozzarella on top, season.

Bake in the oven for about 20 minutes.

PIZZA TOAST

Servings:4

INGREDIENTS

- 4 Schb   White bread
- 1 Tbsp   butter
- 2 Pc   tomatoes
- 4 Pc Anchovy fillets
- 4 Schb   Emmentaler processed cheese
- 4 Pc Olives

PREPARATION

Toast white bread on both sides, butter on one side, cover with thin tomato slices, and spread the anchovy fillets on top.

Cover with a slice of cheese each.

Slice olives and place on top of the cheese.

Baked in the oven or under the grill for 8-10 minutes until the cheese melts creamy

HAM PIZZA

Servings:4

INGREDIENTS

- 450 G Flour
- 0.5 Wf   Germ
- 4 Tbsp   olive oil
- 1 TL   salt
- 1 prize   sugar
- 200 ml   lukewarm water
- 1 Tbsp   Flour to work out
- 2 Tbsp   Oil for the tin
- 12 Schb Ham
- 1 Glass   Tomato pesto
- 4 Pc   Garlic cloves

- 2 Tbsp   Olive oil (topping)
- 300 G grated pizza cheese

PREPARATION

Preheat the oven to 230 ° top / bottom heat. Crumble the yeast in a bowl, stir with sugar and water until smooth. Add the flour, olive oil and salt and knead everything into a smooth dough. Cover and let rise in a warm place for about 1 hour.

Shape the dough into 4 balls, roll out into round flat cakes approx. 26 cm in diameter on a little flour and place on 4 oiled baking trays.

Spread half of the tomato pesto on the bottom, spread the cheese on top, cover with ham and drizzle the second half of the tomato pesto on top.

Peel and chop the garlic cloves and mix with the oil, coat the pizza edge thickly with it and distribute the rest on the pizza. Put the pizza in the oven and bake for 15 minutes

PIZZA DOUGH FOR PIZZA STONE

Servings:4

INGREDIENTS

- 500 G Flour type 00 (pizza flour)
- 0.5 Wf   Fresh yeast
- 50 ml warm water (for pre-dough)
- 150 ml   warm water
- 100 ml   milk
- 0.5 TL   sugar
- 15 G sea-salt
- 2 Tbsp   olive oil

PREPARATION

Preheat the oven to 30 degrees top / bottom heat. Sift all of the flour.

For the pre-dough: dissolve the yeast with 50 ml of warm water and 1/2 teaspoon of sugar in a bowl. Add 3 tablespoons of flour to the yeast / sugar / water mixture and stir into the pre-dough. Cover and let the pre-dough rise in the preheated oven for 30 minutes.

For the pizza dough: put the flour in the mixing bowl and prepare a well. Pour the pre-dough, the 150ml water and the milk into the prepared well and stir briefly.

Then add the olive oil and sea salt and knead for about 3 minutes with the dough hook of the food processor. While kneading, check the consistency again and again, if the dough is very dry, a little water can be added.

Put the dough in a bowl dusted with flour and let rise in a warm place (max. 30 degrees) for approx. 2 hours.

Before preparing the pizzas, knead the dough well again and divide it into 4 parts. The pizza can now be shaped and topped as desired.

SPAGHETTI PIZZA FROM THE TRAY

Servings:4

INGREDIENTS

- 2 Pc   onion
- 3 Pc   paprika
- 400 ml   Whipped cream
- 1 Pk   cooked ham
- 5 Pc   tomatoes
- 1 Tbsp   oil
- 3 Tbsp   Tomato paste
- 500 G spaghetti
- 200 G Cheese (grated)

- 1 prize   pepper
- 1 prize   salt

PREPARATION

Cook the spaghetti in salted water according to the instructions on the packet until al dente. Meanwhile, cut the onions, tomatoes and peppers into cubes and sauté them with the oil in a high pan until they are soft. Deglaze everything with the whipped cream. Let it simmer until the sauce thickens. Then season with tomato paste until it has a nice color.

Spread the finished spaghetti on a baking sheet. Top with the cooked ham cubes. Pour the sauce over it and finally spread the grated cheese on top.

Bake at 180 ° C (top / bottom heat) for about 15 minutes, until the cheese has melted and the sauce has absorbed.

PIZZA MUFFINS WITH PUFF PASTRY

Servings:12

INGREDIENTS

- 250 G Minced meat
- 1 Pk   Puff pastry (refrigerated shelf)
- 1 Pc   onion
- 1 Pc   Eggs
- 1 Tbsp   Pizza seasoning
- 2 Tbsp   Tomato paste
- 2 Tbsp   Basil (frozen)

PREPARATION

For the pizza muffins with puff pastry, first preheat the oven to 200 degrees top / bottom heat and line a muffin tin with paper liners.

Roll out the puff pastry and cut into 12 squares. Now use the pastry sheets to lay out the paper cases.

Then peel and finely chop the onion. Mix the onion, minced meat, egg, pizza seasoning and tomato paste in a bowl. Now spread the mixture into the prepared dough molds.

Sprinkle with a lot of cheese and bake in the oven for 30 minutes.

PIZZA WITH ANCHOVIES AND CAPERS

Servings:2

INGREDIENTS

- 350 G Flour
- 180 ml   Water, lukewarm
- 20 ml oil
- 4 G   Germ
- 2 TL salt
- for the topping
- 250 ml   Polpa
- 80 G Cheese, grated
- 80 G Mozzarella

- 3 Tbsp   Capers
- 100 G Pickled anchovies
- 70 G arugula
- 2 Pc Garlic cloves
- 1 prize   salt
- 1 prize   pepper

preparation

For the dough: dissolve the yeast with water and icing sugar. Then mix water, oil and salt with yeast (a food processor is well suited for this). Now knead in the flour in parts.

Knead everything until you get a smooth dough, then form a smooth ball of dough. Cover it with cling film and let it rest for at least 2.5 hours (or preferably overnight).

Divide the pizza dough into 2 parts, roll out both with a little grippy flour and place on 2 baking sheets lined with baking paper. Finally, top the pizzas with sliced cheese and finish with anchovies, capers and rocket. Bake the two pizzas one behind the other on the lowest setting for about 5 minutes.

CURD PIZZA DOUGH

Servings:1

INGREDIENTS

- 200 G Curd cheese (20%)
- 1 Pc egg
- 4 Tbsp milk
- 8 Tbsp oil
- 1 Msp salt
- 200 G Whole wheat flour
- 0.5 Pk baking powder

PREPARATION

For the quark pizza dough, knead a dough from curd cheese, milk, egg, oil, salt, flour and baking powder. Roll the dough onto a baking sheet lined with parchment paper and cover to taste.

PERFECT PIZZA

Servings:3

INGREDIENTS

- 500 G Flour
- 300 ml   warm water
- 1.5 TL salt
- 15 G   Germ
- 100 G handy flour for the work surface
- 0.5 Glass   Tomato paste for spreading
- 3 Pk   Buffalo mozzarella
- 1 prize   basil
- 1 prize   oregano

PREPARATION

First, the flour is sifted into the food processor. Then the salt is added. Dissolve the yeast in the water and add.

Then knead the ingredients into a homogeneous dough. Long kneading of at least 30 minutes is required so that the dough is nice and elastic.

After kneading, cover the dough with a damp cloth and let rise for at least an hour. Then divide the dough into three parts.

Dust the work surface vigorously with the handy wheat flour and roll out or pull out the dough thinly, but always make sure that there is enough flour on the dough and on the work surface.

Preheat the oven to 250 ° C hot air and let the tray on which the pizza is placed heat up, so that the base of the pizza will also be nice and crispy.

Place the pizza on baking paper, top with tomato paste, basil and - or oregano and mozzarella. Then place the pizza with the baking paper on the hot tray, the pizza is best when you only have one in the oven at a time. Bake for about 5 minutes.

ASPARAGUS PIZZA

Servings:4

INGREDIENTS

- 500 G Asparagus (green)
- 1 cups Whipped cream
- 0.5 cups creme fraiche Cheese
- 1 Pc   carrot
- 1 Msp nutmeg
- 100 G broccoli
- 100 G Cheese (grated)
- 1 Pk   Pizza dough (cooling compartment)
- 3 Tbsp   Tomato sauce
- 1 prize   pepper
- 1 prize   salt

PREPARATION

For the asparagus pizza, first preheat the oven to 200 degrees and line a baking sheet with baking paper. Roll out the pizza dough on the baking paper and pull the edges up a little.

Then wash the asparagus, if necessary cut off the hard ends. Spread the asparagus on the dough. Spread the broccoli florets on top. Clean and slice the carrots.

Mix the sour cream, tomato sauce and creme fraiche, season with salt, pepper and nutmeg. Spread this mixture on the dough. Spread the carrot pieces on top as well. Spread the asparagus in the same way.

Bake in the preheated oven for 30 minutes.

PIZZA "CARBONARA"

Servings:2

INGREDIENTS

- 3 Pc yolk
- 250 G ham
- 1 cups Whipped cream
- 100 G Paprika, green
- 50 G butter
- 1 prize   salt
- 1 prize   pepper
- for the pizza dough
- 350 G Flour
- 175 ml   Water, lukewarm
- 20 ml oil

- 4 G   Germ
- 9 G   salt

PREPARATION

First dissolve the yeast with water and icing sugar. Then mix water, oil and salt with yeast. Now knead in the flour in parts.

Knead everything until you get a smooth dough, then form a smooth ball of dough. Cover it with cling film and let it rest for at least 2.5 hours (or preferably overnight).

In the meantime, cut the ham and paprika into strips and briefly toast them in butter in a non-stick pan. Add whipped cream and bring to the boil briefly; Take the pan off the heat and thicken with the yolk. Now bind the mixture with a little flour and season with salt and pepper.

Roll out the dough into the desired shape on a floured surface and distribute the carbonara sauce evenly on top. Then bake in a preheated oven at 180 ° C for about 20 minutes.

ROCKET PIZZA

Servings:4

INGREDIENTS

- 1 Pc   Pizza dough (ready)
- 150 G arugula
- 175 G Cream cheese (herbs)
- 2 Tbsp   Pine nuts
- 4 TL   olive oil

PREPARATION

Preheat the oven to 180 ° C (convection). Divide the
pizza dough into 4 parts, shape into balls, roll out and
place on two baking sheets lined with baking paper.

Sort out the rocket, wash it, dry it well and, if you like, pick or cut into bite-sized pieces.

Brush the pizza dough with cream cheese, sprinkle with the pine nuts and season with pepper, then bake in the oven for about 15 minutes. Take the pizzas out of the oven and top with the rocket. Drizzle with 1 teaspoon of olive oil, season with salt and pepper to taste and serve immediately.

TOMATO PIZZA

Servings:1

INGREDIENTS

- Pc Pizza dough (according to the basic recipe)
- 10 branch   Thyme (fresh)
- 2 Pc   Garlic cloves
- 3 Pc   tomatoes
- 1 prize   pepper
- 4 Tbsp   Olive oil (qualitative)
- 1 prize   salt
- 60 G Tomato sauce
- 100 G Cheese (vegan)

PREPARATION

Put the homemade, prepared pizza dough on a baking sheet and shape. Preheat the oven to 250 ° C.

Then the topping is prepared: finely chop the thyme leaves and finely chop the garlic. Cut the tomatoes crosswise into 1 cm thick slices.

First spread the tomato sauce on the dough. Then put the cheese (vegan) and the tomato slices on the dough. Then season with plenty of pepper and sprinkle with thyme and garlic. Now drizzle with a little olive oil.

The pizza is then placed in the preheated oven and baked at 250 degrees on the lowest rack for 15 to 20 minutes. Put fresh basil leaves on the pizza as a decoration before serving.

PIZZA PEST STICK

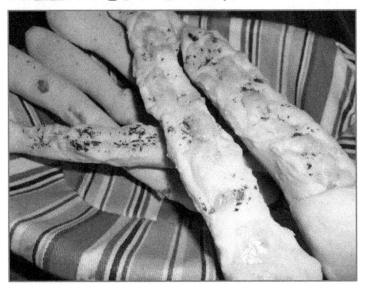

Servings:4

INGREDIENTS

- 1 Pc   finished pizza dough
- 0.5 Glass   Basil pesto
- 0.5 Pk grated mountain cheese

PREPARATION

Place the finished pizza dough (bought or made yourself) on a floured work surface. Cut out strips approx. 2 cm thick.

Spread the pesto and cheese on the strips as desired and roll up or fold up.

Bake the sticks in the oven at about 200 degrees for 13-15 minutes.

TUNA PIZZA

Servings:4

INGREDIENTS

- 1 Pk   Pizza dough (cooling shelf)
- 1 Can Tomatoes (diced)
- 3 Tbsp   Tomato paste
- 2 Can tuna
- 1 Pc   onion
- 150 G Mushrooms
- 1 Pc   paprika
- 1 prize   salt
- 1 Tbsp   oil
- 150 G Cheese (grated)
- 1 Pa   black olives

PREPARATION

For the tuna pizza, preheat the oven to 200 degrees top / bottom heat and roll out the pizza dough on a baking sheet. Brush the dough with a little oil.

Then peel the onion and cut into rings. Clean the mushrooms and cut into slices, wash the peppers, remove the seeds and cut into bite-sized pieces, core the olives and cut into slices. Drain the tuna in a colander.

Mix the tomato paste and tomatoes and spread on the dough, season a little salt. Then put the tuna, onion, mushrooms, paprika and finally the cheese on the pizza.

Bake the pizza in the oven for about 30 minutes until the cheese has melted.

PIZZA WITH ANCHOVIES

Servings:4

INGREDIENTS

- 500 G Flour
- 15 G yeast
- 1 TL salt
- 0.5 Water (warm)
- 3 Tbsp olive oil
- 100 G Olives (black)
- 150 G Anchovies
- 1 Pc Onions

PREPARATION

Crumble the yeast, add a little lukewarm water and let it rest for 5 minutes. Pile up the flour and make a well in the middle.

Put the water, the olive oil and the salt in it. Knead all ingredients well until you get an elastic and smooth dough. Then shape the dough into a ball, wrap it in a clean kitchen towel and let rise in a warm place for 2 hours.

Then knead the dough again for 1-2 minutes, divide it into four parts and let it rest for another 15 minutes.

Now shape four 1/2 cm thick round pizza bases, brush with olive oil and cover with the anchovies. Place on a baking sheet and bake for 15 minutes in the oven preheated to 190 ° C top / bottom heat.

ARTICHOKE PIZZA

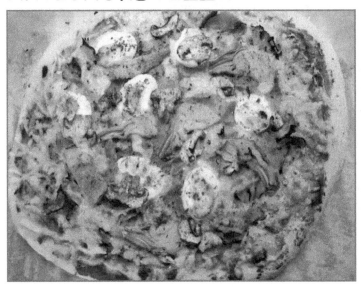

Servings:3

INGREDIENTS

- 500 G Flour
- 1 TL salt
- 1 Pk Dry yeast
- 1 TL sugar
- 300 ml water
- 150 G Tomato sauce
- 300 G Pizza cheese
- 1 prize Pizza seasoning
- 3 Pc Eggs (cooked)
- 1 Glass artichokes

PREPARATION

Knead the flour, salt, sugar, dry yeast and water into a dough and cover in a bowl and let rise for 30 minutes.

Place the dough on a lightly floured work surface and divide into three pieces. Press the dough balls a little flat with your hand and carefully pull them apart.

Brush the round dough with tomato sauce, then sprinkle with pizza cheese. Cut the ham, artichokes and eggs into slices, cover with them and finally sprinkle with pizza seasoning. Bake in the oven at 220 degrees until crispy.

FAST PIZZA DOUGH

Servings:1

INGREDIENTS

- 5 Tbsp   milk
- 7 Tbsp   olive oil
- 250 G Potting
- 1 Pk   baking powder
- 1 TL   salt
- 1 Pc   egg
- 400 G Flour smooth)

PREPARATION

For the quick pizza dough, knead a smooth dough from curd cheese, milk, oil, salt, egg, flour and baking powder.

Line a baking sheet with parchment paper, roll out the dough and cover to taste. Bake for about 35 minutes in the oven at 180 degrees.

PIZZA WITH SPINACH AND PINE NUTS

Servings:4

INGREDIENTS

- 1 Wf Dry yeast
- 250 G unbleached flour
- 0.5 TL   salt
- 180 ml   lukewarm water
- 6 Tbsp   extra virgin olive oil
- 4 Pc   Cloves of garlic, finely chopped
- 1 Tbsp   fresh rosemary
- 2 TL salt
- 375 G spinach

- 100 G Sultanas
- 30 G roasted pine nuts
- 1 prize   salt
- 1 prize   freshly ground pepper

PREPARATION

Sift the flour, yeast, and salt into the bowl of the food processor. Add water and 2 tablespoons of olive oil and mix all ingredients together well in short intervals.

Knead vigorously by hand for 2 minutes. Let the dough clap hard on the work surface several times, this strengthens the so-called dough structure. Oil the dough ball a little and cover and let rise in a warm place - about 4 hours -

In the meantime, wash and sort the spinach thoroughly several times and only put it on with the drained water at a medium temperature. Cook with the sultanas and pine nuts until it is just firm to the bite. Stir in the oil and season with salt and pepper.

Knead the pizza dough again and roll it out into an oblong rectangle. Make indentations in the dough with your fingers, sprinkle with garlic, rosemary and salt and drizzle with the remaining olive oil.

Bake on lightly oiled baking paper at approx. 200 ° C for about 20-30 minutes, until the pizza has a nice, light brown crust.

Let cool down a little and top with the spinach mixture.

AMERICAN PIZZA

Servings:2

INGREDIENTS

- 350 G Flour smooth
- 175 ml   Water, lukewarm
- 17 ml olive oil
- 4 G   Germ
- 9 G   salt
- for the topping
- 0.125 Tomato polpa
- 50 G Chorizo
- 150 G Cheddar
- 6 Pc Jalapeños
- 2 Pc Garlic cloves, peeled and finely chopped

- 0.5 TL   salt
- 1 prize   pepper
- 18 Bl basil

PREPARATION

For the dough, dissolve the yeast in the water. Then mix the oil and salt with the yeast. Now add the flour and knead everything into a smooth dough. Wrap the dough in cling film and let it rest for at least 2.5 hours (or preferably overnight).

Preheat the oven to 220 degrees and prepare the ingredients for the topping: to do this, season the tomato polpa with garlic, salt and pepper; Cut the chorizo into pieces, grate the cheddar, wash the jalapenos and cut into rings.

Divide the pizza dough into two parts, roll it out with a little grippy flour and place on two baking sheets lined with baking paper. Top with polpa, chorizo, cheddar and jalapenos.

Let the pizza rise for another 10 minutes and then bake for 10-15 minutes until the desired brown color and garnish with basil leaves before serving.

PIZZA WITH BRESAOLA AND ARUGULA

Servings:2

INGREDIENTS

- 250 G Pizza flour (or plain wheat flour)
- 125 ml   Water (lukewarm)
- 0.5 Wf   Germ (fresh)
- 1 prize   sugar
- 3 Tbsp   olive oil
- 0.5 TL   salt
- 1 Cup Flour for dusting
- 250 G ricotta
- 50 G Parmesan (grated)

- 1 Federation arugula
- 200 G Bresaola (Italian beef ham) in slices

PREPARATION

For the pizza dough, dissolve the yeast and sugar in lukewarm water and knead with the flour, 1 tablespoon of olive oil and salt to form a dough. Shape the dough into a ball, place on a floured board, dust with a little flour and cover with cling film and leave to rest until the dough has risen to double its size.

Then roll out the dough thinly, brush with ricotta, sprinkle with parmesan and drizzle with the remaining olive oil.

To bake the pizza, bring the pizza stone in the oven to the highest possible temperature, place the pizza on top and bake for 3 to 4 minutes until crispy.

Wash the rocket and spin dry. Take the finished pizza out of the oven, cover with rocket and bresaola slices and drizzle with a little olive oil.

PIZZA MARGHERITA

Servings:4

INGREDIENTS

- 300 G Flour
- 0.5 Wf   Germ
- 1 TL sugar
- 1 TL salt
- 125 ml   milk
- 125 ml   water
- 1 Tbsp   oil
- 150 ml   Tomatoes, happened
- 1 Can Corn
- 2 Pc tomatoes
- 1 Pk Pizza cheese

- 1 Tbsp   Pizza seasoning

PREPARATION

Dig a well in the flour for the yeast dough and crumble the yeast. Spread the sugar on the yeast and pour 1 tablespoon of warm water into the pit. Warm the milk and water and add to the flour. Add oil and salt and mix well with a dough hook. If the dough is too sticky, add a little more flour.

Let the yeast dough rise in a warm place for about 20 minutes. Pour some oil onto a baking sheet and spread the batter on it.

Brush the dough with tomato paste and distribute all the other ingredients on the dough. Finally sprinkle the pizza seasoning and place in the oven at 160 ° C for about 20 minutes.

PIZZA STRUDEL

Servings:4

INGREDIENTS

- 1 Pk puff pastry
- 2 Pc tomatoes
- 100 GCheese, grated
- 80 G ham
- 1 Can Corn
- 0.5 Stg leek
- 1 TL Pizza seasoning

PREPARATION

Roll out the puff pastry. Cut the tomatoes into slices and place about two thirds on the puff pastry.

In a bowl, mix the ham cut into strips, leek, grated cheese, corn (to taste) and pizza seasoning and spread over the tomatoes. Place the remaining tomatoes on top.

Fold up the puff pastry and bake in the oven on a baking sheet at 200 ° C for about 20 minutes.

PISSALADIERS

Servings:10

INGREDIENTS

- 350 G Flour (sifted)
- 0.5 Wf yeast
- 2 Tbsp olive oil
- 1 TL salt
- 100 G Olives (black)
- 16 Pc Anchovy fillets (in oil)

for the topping

- 1 kg Onions
- 4 Tbsp olive oil
- 1 prize salt

- 1 prize   pepper
- 6 Stg thyme

PREPARATION

For the dough, sieve the flour into a bowl and form a hollow in the middle. Crumble the yeast in a small bowl, mix with 180 milliliters of lukewarm water and finally add to the flour trough with oil and salt. Knead everything vigorously until you get a smooth dough. Then let rise in a warm place for about 60 minutes.

Now we come to the topping: cut the onions into fine strips. Heat the oil in a saucepan and fry the onions in it over medium heat until golden brown, then season with salt and pepper. While the onions are cooling, pluck the thyme leaves from the stems and chop finely. Then add to the onions.

Now preheat the oven to 200 ° C. In addition, cut the olives from the stone and drain the anchovy fillets in a sieve.

Now knead the dough well on a floured work surface and divide it into 4 equal pieces. Each piece is then rolled out 2 to 3 mm thin, pierced several times with a fork and brushed with a little oil. Then spread the onion mixture on the flatbread. As soon as everything is covered (except the edge), the cakes come one after the other in the oven and are baked until crispy in about 5 to 10 minutes.

Cover the finished flatbreads with anchovies and olives
- done!

TUNA PIZZA

Servings:4

INGREDIENTS

- 1 Pk   Pizza dough (cooling shelf)
- 1 Can Tomatoes (diced)
- 3 Tbsp   Tomato paste
- 2 Can tuna
- 1 Pc   onion
- 150 G Mushrooms
- 1 Pc   paprika
- 1 prize   salt
- 1 Tbsp   oil
- 150 G Cheese (grated)
- 1 Pa   black olives

PREPARATION

For the tuna pizza, preheat the oven to 200 degrees top / bottom heat and roll out the pizza dough on a baking sheet. Brush the dough with a little oil.

Then peel the onion and cut into rings. Clean the mushrooms and cut into slices, wash the peppers, remove the seeds and cut into bite-sized pieces, core the olives and cut into slices. Drain the tuna in a colander.

Mix the tomato paste and tomatoes and spread on the dough, season a little salt. Then put the tuna, onion, mushrooms, paprika and finally the cheese on the pizza.

Bake the pizza in the oven for about 30 minutes until the cheese has melted.

PIZZA WITH PUFF PASTRY

Servings:2

INGREDIENTS

- 1 Pc   Puff pastry (ready)
- 6 Tbsp   Tomato paste
- 10 G ham
- 10 G salami
- 5 Pc Chili peppers
- 4 Pc pineapple
- 1 Can Tuna fish
- 1 prize   oregano
- 1 prize   pepper
- 1 prize salt

PREPARATION

Roll out the puff pastry on a baking sheet and brush with the tomato paste.

Spread the ham, salami, peppers, pineapple and tuna on the dough and season with oregano, salt and pepper. Bake in the preheated oven at approx. 180 ° C for about 20 minutes.

PIZZA STRUDEL

Servings:4

INGREDIENTS

- 1 Pk   puff pastry
- 2 Pc   tomatoes
- 100 G Cheese, grated
- 80 G ham
- 1 Can Corn
- 0.5 Stg   leek
- 1 TL   Pizza seasoning

PREPARATION

Roll out the puff pastry. Cut the tomatoes into slices and place about two thirds on the puff pastry.

In a bowl, mix the ham cut into strips, leek, grated cheese, corn (to taste) and pizza seasoning and spread over the tomatoes. Place the remaining tomatoes on top.

Fold up the puff pastry and bake in the oven on a baking sheet at 200 ° C for about 20 minutes.

POLENTA PIZZA

Servings:1

INGREDIENTS

- 100 G Polentagries coarse
- 300 ml   water
- 100 ml   milk
- 150 G Tomato sauce
- 100 G Carrots
- 100 G leek
- 100 G cauliflower
- 150 G Mountain cheese (grated)
- 50 G Onions
- 5 G   oregano
- 1 Msp nutmeg

- 1 prize   pepper
- 1 prize salt

PREPARATION

Boil the polenta with water, milk, salt, pepper and nutmeg in a saucepan and spread on a baking sheet, allow to cool a little.

In the meantime, wash, clean and chop the vegetables. Brush the cooled mass with tomato sauce and top with the vegetables.

Sprinkle with cheese, onions and oregano and bake at about 160 ° C for about 25 minutes.

PIZZA SALAMI

Servings:4

INGREDIENTS

- 1 Pc   Pizza dough to stir
- 1 Can Diced tomatoes
- 1 Tbsp   Oregano, dried
- 1 prize   salt
- 1 prize   pepper
- 130 ml   water
- 100 G Salami slices
- 120 G Mozzarella
- 0.5 TL   sugar
- 2 Tbsp   olive oil
- 4 Tbsp   Olives, black, pitted

- 1 Pc   onion

PREPARATION

Preheat the oven to 250 ° C.

Peel the onion and cut into cubes. Peel and finely chop the clove of garlic. Let the olive oil get hot in a pan and steam the onion cubes in it until translucent. Mix in the garlic and sugar and cook for another 2 minutes.

Mix the oregano with the pizza tomatoes, place in a saucepan and heat. Season with salt and pepper and simmer gently for 4 minutes.

Knead the contents of the pizza dough bag with 125 ml of lukewarm water. Flour the work surface and roll out 2 circles of about 22 cm. Place these on the baking sheet.

Drain the mozzarella and cut into cubes. Spread the tomato sauce on the dough base, then top with salami and olives. Spread the cheese cubes on top.

Place in the oven for 15 minutes on the lower rack.

PIZZA GUGELHUPF

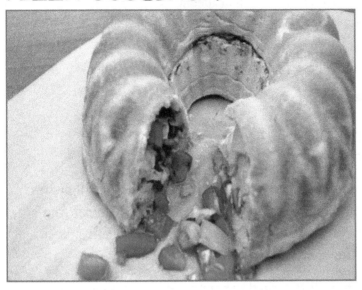

Servings:4

INGREDIENTS

- 1 kg Yeast dough (according to the basic recipe)
- 5 Pc Cocktail tomatoes
- 1 Pc onion
- 1 Pc leek
- 200 G cheese
- 1 prize   salt
- 100 G Tomato paste (or ketchup)
- 2 Tbsp   sour cream
- 2 Pc Bell pepper (à red, yellow, green)
- 100 G Ham sausage

- 1 Tbsp   Butter (for the mold)
- 1 prize   marjoram
- 1 prize   oregano
- 1 prize   Basil (dried)
- 1 Pc   Clove of garlic (fresh, crushed)

PREPARATION

Prepare a yeast dough for the pizza jelly cake according to the basic recipe .

Peel and dice the onion. Cut the leek into small pieces. Wash tomatoes and cut into small pieces. Wash the peppers (yellow, red, green) and cut into fine pieces. Cut the ham sausage into small pieces.

Now put all the finely chopped ingredients in a bowl and season well with marjoram, oregano, basil, salt and garlic.

Then cut (or grate) the cheese. Meanwhile, mix the tomato paste with the sour cream in a small bowl and set aside.

Now brush a Gugelhupf pan with butter and line the pan with the pizza dough - cut off the dough hanging over it with a knife.

Now spread the dough with the tomato and sour cream sauce. Then fill with the vegetables.

Finally, put the cheese on top and cover the filling with the remaining pizza dough - press the edges together well.

Bake in the preheated oven at 220 ° C for approx. 25 minutes, middle rack. Switch back to 200 ° C for the last 10 minutes.

Turn out of the mold while it is still hot and serve.

PAN PIZZA FROM AMERICA

Servings:2

INGREDIENTS

- 250 G Minced meat
- 150 G Mushrooms
- 200 G tomatoes
- 2 Pc paprika
- 1 Tbsp   Thyme (dried)
- 150 G Mozzarella
- 100 G Parmesan (grated)
- 1 Glass   Pizza sauce

for the dough

- 150 G Flour

- 1 prize   salt
- 1 Tbsp   olive oil
- 0.5 Pk Germ
- 70 ml water

PREPARATION

For pan pizza from America, first prepare the batter. Sift the flour into a bowl, pour salt and olive oil over it and mix with a fork. Make a hollow in the middle and crumble the yeast. Gradually add the lukewarm water until a smooth dough has formed. Let rise in a warm place for 25 minutes.

Preheat the oven to 200 degrees. Brush a pan with oil, roll out the dough, place it in the pan and pull it up on the edge. Wash tomatoes and peppers and cut into small pieces. Clean and quarter the mushrooms. Cut the mozzarella into slices.

Briefly fry the minced meat in a pan with oil. Brush the dough with pizza sauce and spread the minced meat on top. Now cover with the prepared vegetables and cover with mozzarella and parmesan. Sprinkle with thyme.

Bake in the oven for about 25 minutes until the cheese has melted.

TOAST PIZZA

Servings:2

INGREDIENTS

- 4 Pc Millet toast
- 5 Tbsp   Tomato sauce (organic, seasoned)
- 2 Tbsp   Corn
- 2 Tbsp   Mushrooms
- 2 Tbsp   paprika
- 6 Tbsp   Cheese (grated)
- 1 prize   oregano

PREPARATION

First preheat the oven to 200 ° C.

Toast the millet toast, then brush with the organic tomato sauce. Spread the corn, mushrooms, peppers, etc. on top. Sprinkle with the grated cheese. Possibly oregano and marjoram on top and then into the pipe.

Baked in the oven at 200 ° C until the cheese has melted and has got a light color.

MINI CALZONE

Servings:10

INGREDIENTS

- 1 Pc   Pizza dough (basic recipe or frozen)
- 150 G Mushrooms
- 2 prize   pepper
- 2 prize   salt
- 1 prize   oregano
- 200 G Cocktail tomatoes
- 2 Tbsp   Creme fraiche Cheese
- 125 G Mozzarella
- 1 Pc   clove of garlic
- 1 TL   Lemon juice

PREPARATION

First cover a baking sheet with baking paper, roll out the pizza dough and cut out 12 circles with a round biscuit cutter (10 cm diameter) and then place them on the sheet. Preheat the oven to 200 degrees top / bottom heat.

Then wash the mushrooms, dab and cut into thin slices. Wash and quarter the tomatoes too. Drain the mozzarella and cut into small cubes.

Then season the creme fraiche with salt, pepper and lemon juice. Peel and finely chop the garlic and fold into the creme fraiche.

Now spread the cream on the pizza circles. Spread the mushrooms, tomatoes and mozzarella on only half of the pizza circles and beat together to make small calzone pizzas.

Sprinkle with salt, pepper and oregano again as you like. Bake in the hot oven (lower rack) for about 15 minutes.

PIZZA BOAT

Servings:6

INGREDIENTS

- 600 G Spelled flour
- 1 Pk   Dry yeast
- 1 TL   sugar
- 3 TL   salt
- 300 ml   lukewarm water
- 5 Tbsp   olive oil
- 3 Tbsp   tomato ketchup
- 24 Schb salami
- 1 Can Corn
- 1 Pc   Red pepper
- 100 G grated cheese

- 2 TL oregano

PREPARATION

Sift the flour into a bowl, add the dry yeast, sugar, olive oil, salt and water and work into a smooth dough. Let rest for an hour.

Then divide it into 6 pieces, pull them out in your hand, place them on a tray, fold in the edges and shape them into a ship.

Brush with tomato ketchup, spread the salami, cheese, diced paprika and corn on top and season with oregano. Place on a baking sheet and bake at 230 degrees for about 20 minutes.

PIZZA CON FRUTTI DI MARE

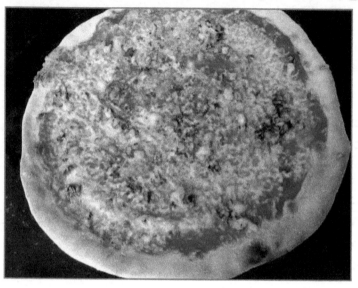

Servings:2

INGREDIENTS

- 125 ml   Tomato sauce
- 100 G Gouda cheese (grated)
- Bullet Mozzarella (grated)
- 150 G Scallops (just the meat)
- 60 G   Anchovies
- 2 Pc   Cloves of garlic (freshly squeezed)

for the dough

- 500 G Flour smooth)
- 220 ml   Water (lukewarm)
- 2 Tbsp   olive oil

- 1 Pk   Dry yeast
- 1 TL   salt
- 1 prize   Granulated sugar

PREPARATION

For the dough: sift the flour into a bowl. Mix the water (lukewarm) in another bowl with the salt, a pinch of sugar, the yeast and the oil, then slowly add the flour.

Knead everything with a dough hook of a food processor until you get a smooth dough and form a smooth ball of dough. Cover this with a kitchen towel and let it rest for at least 40 minutes at room temperature.

After the rest time, divide the pizza dough into 2 parts, roll out both with a little grippy flour and place on 2 baking sheets lined with baking paper.

Finally, brush the dough with the tomato sauce and top with mussels, Gouda cheese, anchovies and mozzarella. Bake the two pizzas one behind the other on the middle rack for approx. 20 minutes with hot air at 170 ° C.

CONCLUSION

Pizza is certainly the best-known and for many also the most popular dish from Italy. The flatbread from the Neapolitan cuisine made its triumphant advance on the menus of the world at the beginning of the 19th century.

The most important thing in a pizza recipe is to use the right pizza dough and fresh ingredients for the topping. But the right baking time and the right baking device (pizza oven) should not be neglected either - here you will find a selection of pizza recipes that are easy to make yourself.

Lightning Source UK Ltd.
Milton Keynes UK
UKHW020656240521
384264UK00005B/200